Reflections in Silhouette

Poems

Reflections in Silhouette
Poems

T. L. Cooper

DEDICATION

I dedicate this book of poetry to the friends and family who loved me for my
true self even when I lost track of who that was.
My love for you is unconditional, heartfelt, and everlasting.
Thank you!

ACKNOWLEDGMENTS

The poems between these covers come from life, and therefore I must acknowledge all the people who've played a role in my life because they've each contributed to the woman I've become. I thank them for providing fuel, ammunition, and weaponry for the words that have helped me discover passion, inspiration, and insight in life as well as my place in the world.

As always, I offer my gratitude and love to Loay Abu-Husein for his support and love! Without his skill, knowledge, and talent, this book cover wouldn't exist.

Many thanks and love to friends, Kelly Deaton, Lori Felmey, and Bryan Rader for their feedback on both individual poems and the cover. Their time, attention to detail, honesty, and friendship enrich not only my writing but my life! Thanks for reminding me that revealing what makes me feel most vulnerable may help someone else and is therefore the strength of my work.

Authors, Stacey Rourke, Joanne Pence, Pari Noskin Taichert, and LJ Sellers earned my eternal gratitude with thoughtful, honest, thought provoking and helpful comments regarding myriad aspects of the book.

Many thanks to all those who've read my poems and offered encouragement over the years!

Never to be forgotten are the friends and family who offer me their undying support and unconditional love as I grow into the best me I can be.

Many thanks to you for reading my work! May you find something in these pages that speaks to you on your journey to become your best self!

Evolving

Who I am
Today
May differ from the person remembered from
Yesterday
And likely won't be the person encountered in
Future days

Remnants may remain
Those bits that create change
Those scars that teach lessons
To remind of the journey and the destination
To provide familiarity

Vague impressions may surface
Of times past
Of laughter and tears
Of joy and heartbreak
Of moments shared

Tiny fragments of physical and emotional touch
Creating connection
Melding moments into lifetimes
Pulling apart to find new beginnings
Leaving traces that forever remind

Who I am
Today
May differ from the person remembered from
Yesterday
And likely won't be the person encountered in
Future days

Laid Bare

I stand before you
Presenting all I am
Nothing more, nothing less
Battle scars and smiles
Bruised heart and laughs
Broken soul and forgiveness
Too harsh with words at times
Too sensitive for my own good
Blind with determination
Afraid to succeed
Dreams of a perfect life
Doubtful of anything too good
Embracing the future
Hiding from the past
Needing too much
Independent to a fault
Loving fully
Pushing love away
Too trusting
Not trusting myself
I stand before you
Risking all I am
You smile at me
Open your heart
Embrace me with your arms
Accept all I am
Nothing more, nothing less
Letting me grow
Holding me tight and setting me free
Loving me in spite of and because of
Reaching out when I pull back

Encouraging my dreams
Keeping me grounded
Holding me together
Letting me fall apart in your arms
Showing me the good in life
Accepting my contradictions
I stand before you
Giving all I am
Grateful to you for all you are
You stand before me
Trusting me to love and accept you
For all you are
I move beside you
You take my hand
We move forward into our life
All that we are
Nothing more, nothing less
But together facing it all
Yesterday, today, tomorrow

Seriously Tempted

I am
Seriously tempted
To be
Your heart's desire
What you want of me

I am
Seriously tempted
To forget
Who I've become
Who I struggle to remain

I am
Seriously tempted
To give
My very being away
My soul to you

I am
Seriously tempted
To become
Merely a shell of me
An empty vessel filled by you

I am
Seriously tempted
To extinguish
The light shining in me
The richness of my thoughts and feelings

I am

Seriously tempted
To kill
The dreams that make me who I am
The goals that give me purpose

I am
Seriously tempted
To surrender
My heart, my soul, my mind
My existence

I am
Seriously tempted
But in the end
The who I am won't allow me
I can only be me

I am
Seriously tempted
But in the end
It would be pretense
It would be torture

I am
Seriously tempted
But in the end
I would hate you
I would despise me

I am
Seriously tempted
But in the end
My anger would take over
My resentment would kill us both

I am
Seriously tempted
But in the end
I can only be me
Even if I disappoint you

I am
Seriously tempted…

The Mask

One day
I put on a mask
To make you love me
Not because you asked
But because I feared
The look in your eyes
Disappointment, I believe it was
So I
Settled the mask into place
Tweaked it
Made it beautiful
Perfected it to make you happy
Created exactly what
Made you smile
Turned the look in your eye to approval
Made you love me
As time passed
I deceived myself
I accepted the mask as
The real me
I forgot who I was under
The mask
When the mask cracked
As they will
I quickly – before anyone could see
Plastered the cracks
Filled in the holes
Blended the paint
Hid the damaged and weakened foundation
Corrected its imperfections
Settled the mask back into place

When the mask slipped
As they will
I quickly – before anyone could see
Pushed it around to make it fit
Smoothed the borders
Adjusted it so you wouldn't notice
Ignored the ever rotting foundation
Pretended its perfection remained
Settled the mask back into place

Your acceptance
Your approval
Your love
For
The mask
Intoxicated me
Into believing
The mask was
Better
Happier
Stronger
More beautiful
Than me
And I began
To forget
I wasn't
The mask
One day
A friend from my past
Reminded me
The person under
The mask was
As acceptable as

As beautiful as
As perfect as
As loveable as
The mask
I resisted
I clung to the mask
The mask had brought me
Protection
Acceptance
Approval
Love
The mask
Began
To itch
To chafe
To strangle
To smother
To kill
You loved
The mask
So very much
I saw it in your eyes
I felt it in your touch
I heard it in your voice
Could you love *me*?
How could I disappoint you?
And yet how could I deny me?
I shoved the mask around
Tried to make it comfortable again
Tried to make it reality again
Tried to deny the mask and I weren't the same
Tried to imagine being without
The mask
Repairs became difficult

The mask crumbles
A little more each day
I fear
What will happen
The day it's destroyed
When I'm only me
When I'm no longer
The mask

Bit by Bit

Bit by bit
I fade into the background
Willing myself forward
But you don't see

Bit by bit
I disintegrate
Struggling to hold on to the pieces
But you don't see

Bit by bit
I fall into an empty chasm
Straining to stay on top
But you don't see

Bit by bit
I sink into the quicksand of life
Reaching up for a lifeline
But you don't see

Bit by bit
I lose myself
Needing to be found
But you don't see

Bit by bit
I gasp for breath
Dying to live
But you don't see

Bit by bit

I let go
I stop fighting
But you don't see…

The Mirror

One day
I stood before
The mirror
I avoided looking in my eyes
The woman looking back at me
Reflected the possibility of the girl I once was
Perhaps even the woman I was before...
Or at least the woman I was destined to be before...
I turned my head
But the woman looking back at me
Refused to let me turn away
She questioned those decisions
The ones that catapulted me on my journey
The ones that pushed aside the woman I dreamed of being
In favor of the acceptable, the loveable, the respectable
woman
Defined by someone else

Yesterday
I stood before
The mirror
Naked, bare, vulnerable
And I looked in my eyes
I stared at the woman looking back at me
Challenged her to show me the truth of me
Begged her for another chance to shine
Relinquished my stubborn fears to her wisdom
Tears filled my eyes
I blinked them back
I reminded myself
There are those who have

Always loved me as is – not as they imagined me to be
Never demanded I lose me to keep them
Never suggested I was anything less than…
Never made me feel I couldn't…
Never stood in my way

I stood before
The mirror
Saw
More than a body
More than a face
More than the sum of my parts
More than my flaws
More than my weaknesses
I looked into my eyes
Saw
The pain
The joy
The strength
The love
All I've given
All I have left to give
All I've received
All I've learned
Saw
Who I was
Who I am
Who I can become – the possibility of me still exists

I looked into
The mirror
Realized
Not all I left behind was bad
Not all I left behind was good

Not all I became was bad
Not all I became was good
Not all I see stings with regret

I look into
The mirror
The woman I am – truly am at the heart of me
Looks out from
The mirror
Screams to be free

Armor

I wear you
Like protective armor
An excuse to keep people out
A reason to avoid closeness
A reason to deny trust
An excuse to reject love

I hide you
Like a shameful transgression
One I didn't commit
One that changes people's view of me
One that creates distance when revealed
One that was thrust upon me

I expose you
Like a bruised secret
To test loyalty
To pretend vulnerability
To make people leave
To hide my truth

I wield you
Like a deadly weapon
To destroy intimacy
To cut out the heart of friendship
To avoid life
To self-destruct

I fight you
Like the invader you are
Because I don't want you

Because I long to be free of you
Because I want the me before you
Because I wish you'd never happened

I cast you aside
Like a thieving intruder
You don't go quietly
You steal the core of me repeatedly without shame
You retreat into the recesses of my life tricking me
You pop back through as soon as I relax my guard

I reluctantly integrate you
Like a disobedient child
Into my life
Into my relationships
Into my thoughts
Into my self

I wear you
Like protective armor
Because you happened to me
Because I can't erase you
Because I'd die if I didn't
Because you are me

Hands

(also appeared in American Poetry Journal and on Associated Content)

Rubbing my back
Caressing my cheek
Holding my hand
Squeezing my shoulder
Rubbing my arm
Pulling me into a hug
Bringing comfort
Smoothing my hair
Brushing my bangs from my eyes
Holding me up
Changing
Pushing me down
Restraining me
Slapping my face
Please don't touch me anymore
No, not there, not like that
Stop
Touching me
Holding me down
Forcing me
Covering my mouth
Finished
Pushing me away
Those hands

Fear

I close my eyes
I see your face
I open my eyes
The sight is gone

I try to sleep
I try not to dream
I try to forget
The memories are there
Always there

I try to cry
But the tears won't come
If they do
Will they ever stop?

I'm scared
Of being alone
I'm scared
Of being with someone, anyone

I fear being vulnerable
Will I ever trust again?

If Only I Hadn't

If only I hadn't
Smiled
Trusted
Befriended

If only I hadn't
Let you in
Said stay and chat a while
Laughed at your jokes

If only I hadn't
Thought of you as a brother
Treasured the friendship you offered
Trusted you as no other

If only I hadn't
Let down my guard
Showed you my true self
Basked in your concern

If only I had
Walked away
Seen the signs
Sensed your obsession

If only I had
Loved myself more
Respected my feelings
Trusted my instincts

Maybe you wouldn't have

If only…

Words

I'm sorry
The words will never be enough
But I long to hear them

You didn't deserve it
The words won't take it away
Though I'd like to hear them

I betrayed you
The words can't erase the pain
Yet hearing them would mean a lot

I know I hurt you
The words can't change the past
Hearing them might release the future

I didn't know what I was doing
The words won't change anything
So why do I want to hear them

I destroyed your ability to trust
The words won't bring back my faith
Hearing them won't restore our friendship

Hurting you was wrong
The words won't fix us
Hearing them would be nice

I don't deserve your forgiveness
The words won't bring peace
So why bother

I know now what I threw away
The words will fall on deaf ears
But please say them, please…

Today I Remembered

Today I remembered
My heart felt at ease
There was no longer pain
My soul found peace
Nothing changed
Except I let go of the fear
I embraced courage
Your hold on me loosened
I broke free
What happened can't be changed
But it no longer defines me
I define myself
The past is simply experience
The present is where I stand
The future represents opportunity

Today I remembered
The person I truly am
The person you tried to harness
The person you tried to alter
The person you pushed to the brink
The person you tried to put in a box with a cute little bow
The person you tried to destroy
The person whose strength was always too much for you
The person who never needed you
The person who was full of hope and ambition

Today I remembered
The good you possessed
And no longer felt guilt in the recognition
You listened

You protected me like a brother
You held me when I cried
You encouraged me to embrace life
You began as my friend

Today I remembered
The hints that something darker lurked below
Your hand imprinting itself on my face with a slap
Forgiving you that because I believed you didn't mean it
Your presence outside my window at three in the morning
Excusing that as protective instead of controlling
You showing up uninvited on my girls' night out
Pretending you didn't know where we were going
Phone calls questioning my whereabouts night and day
Trying to believe it was caring not possessive
Defending you when my friends doubted your intentions

Today I remembered
Your body pinning mine down
My whisper "Is there anything I can do to stop you?"
Your sticky sweet voice and cocky grin as you replied "No"
The pillow falling across my face
An evil I'd never seen on your face paralyzed me
This act I can never forgive

Today I remembered
How afterward you grinned and said
"You need an attitude adjustment."
Knowing how I hated it when my Mom used that reprimand
Knowing every time I heard it I would remember
How you later told me I would "get over it"
How you showed up outside my window again
How I had to move and become unlisted to hide from you
How long it took me to stop looking over my shoulder

How long it took me to take my power back

Today I remembered
And, for the first time
A moment of sadness
For a friendship destroyed
By your hands
By your actions
By my blind trust
By my unwillingness to see the signs

Today I remembered
How that moment
Tainted every happy moment we ever shared
Destroyed relationships that mattered to me
Forced me to stop trusting my judgment
Shattered my self-esteem
Broke my heart
Influenced my decisions for years
Changed who I am forever

Today I remembered
That I'm in control
Of my thoughts
Of my heart
Of my soul
Of my emotions
Of my memories
Of my present
Of my future
Of me

Today I remembered
You have no influence over me

You have no role in my present or future
You only affect me when I allow you
You no longer have the power to create fear in me
You can't hurt me again
You simply don't matter

Today I remembered
I am free to be me
Whoever that me is

You Find Me

What if you find me
I've spent my life
Hiding me from you
Protecting me from you
Running away from you
Building walls to keep you out
Changing my name
Disguising my identity
Arranging and rearranging my life
                          so you can't see me

What if you find me
My heart fears
What you will do
Will you take away my choice
What you will say
Will you silence my voice
What you believe will happen
Will you expect me to welcome you
What you think I owe you
Will you want me to forgive and forget
Who you think I am
        I am no longer your victim

What if you find me
My soul cries
At the prospect
My carefully controlled anger will burst through
My carefully hidden fear will take control of me
My carefully concealed need for vengeance will betray me
My carefully guarded violent fantasies will break me

My carefully created strong, confident persona
will be destroyed
My carefully constructed peaceful, loving self
will disintegrate
My carefully built control
will crumble revealing my fragility
My carefully nurtured security
will explode into vulnerability

What if you find me
My brain freezes
As I consider
The consequences
The potential outcomes
How close you really are
How much I've deceived myself
How I'm not invisible to you
How you might follow through on your promise
– your threat

What if you find me
I relaxed my guard
Publicity I sought
Recognition I desired
I grew tired of hiding
I grew weary of protecting
I grew complacent with the distance of time and space
I needed the world to see me
And deceived myself that you wouldn't
Now my efforts may have revealed me to you

What if you find me

Tears

If the tears would come
I'd let them fall
I feel them in my heart
I hear them in my soul
I think of them
I obsess about them
They threaten my eyes
Yet they can't break free
I fear if the tears came
They'd never stop
My soul, my heart, my mind
Beg me to let them flow
Yet the tightness in my chest
The numbness in my mind
The haunting of my soul
Aren't enough to loosen them
What a relief it would be
To let go
To let them flow
To loosen my control
If they fell
Would my tears
Wash away the numbness
Awaken my fire for life
Or would they
Open old wounds
Awaken anger and sadness
Would either be a relief?
Would either bring clarity?
Would tears be the answer
To my questions
To my concerns
To my fears
Would tears only leave

Dry eyes
Wet cheeks
A runny nose
Tears
I long for them
I need them
Or do I?
What will they really accomplish?
Tears

Something Good

Why can't I see
Why can't I hear
Why can't I smell
Why can't I touch
Why can't I taste
Why can't I feel
Something good

Hiding
Escaping
Just out of reach
Elusive
Unreal
Slipping through my grasp
Something good

Would I even
Recognize
Accept
Appreciate
Acknowledge
Keep
Something good

Memories Swirl

Memories swirl
Like fudge through vanilla ice cream
Blending flavors
Adding texture
Enhancing the experience

Memories swirl
Around in my mind
Haunting my life
Possessing my present
Halting my future

Memories swirl
Around in my heart
Miring me in the past
Tainting my love for others
Choking my love for myself

Memories swirl
Around in my soul
Creating chaos
Destroying my confidence
Stopping my progression

Memories swirl
Around in my being
Shutting out good
Doubts move in
Faults take over

Memories swirl

I halt them
Embrace life
Control today
Create the future I desire

Memories swirl
Around in my mind, heart, soul, & being
Laughter abounds
Smiles replace frowns
Gratitude for all I've learned

Memories swirl
Coming together
The happy, the sad, the indifferent
Components of who I am
Swirled memories

The Voice

Needling, needling
The voice drones on
Never ceasing
Never pausing
Never resting
Moving through the day
The voice never leaves
Relentless criticism
You should be...
You should take care of...
Why aren't you...
You're not doing that right
Call your Mom
Write a story
Edit a book
Clean the house
Write a poem
Don't forget about...
Counting
One, two, three, four....
To stop the voice
Doesn't work
Tortured musings
Relentless guilt
Never perfect
Not even good enough
Do more
Care more
Give more
Too many should be doings
Too many not quite rights

Too many you'll never succeeds
Too many anxieties
The voice constantly reminds
Dwelling on tiny mistakes
Past failures
Endless repetition of wrong words used
The voice
A constant companion
Why can't it say
You're perfect just the way you are
You are loved
You are generous
You don't have to be all to everyone
You don't have to be perfect
You are you
And that's enough
The voice drones on
Endlessly

Things I Will Never Be

Things I will never be
Roles I will never play
Feelings I will never experience
Activities I will never do
The list is long
It might make you sad
You might tell me I'm missing out
To me though it feels like freedom

Things I will never be
Opportunities I refused
People I let walk away
Moments I watched pass
One direction I chose over another
The list is long
It might make you pity me
You might ask me about regrets
I'll tell you about joys

Things I will never be
Some good
Some bad
Some neutral
Some both good and bad
The list is long
It might make you see me as less than
You might tell me those things mean I'm not living
I'll tell you my life is living just as much as yours is

I know a secret
There are many things I am

There are many things I will be
Things you aren't
Things you'll never be

Once Upon a Time

Once upon a time
I believed in
Once upon a time
Happily ever after
A knight on a white horse
Princes rescuing princesses
Poor girls finding out they were princesses
Truth always prevailing
Dishonesty always being exposed
Love conquering all
The promise of sunrises
The magic of sunsets
Friendships lasting forever
People having good intentions
People loving their fellow human beings
People having honest hearts
The American dream
The power of exposing untruths to change lives
The good guys always winning the fight
Justice always being served to the bad guys
The overall good of humanity
Boundless possibilities
Fairy tales
Once upon a time
I believed in
Once upon a time...

The Union

Today I ran into me
Me was playing, smiling, and laughing
I looked like me
Only uptight
I said to me
Why are you so happy?
Me replied, smiling
I have every reason to be
I shook my head
There's too much to do
No time for laughter
No time for this silliness
Me laughed
Without the laughter
You would die
I scolded
There's too much to be done
There's too much to fix in this world
Me looked at I with what could only be pity
So little you've learned
Striving for money
Striving for power
Hiding from love
Running from happiness
I flashed my stubbornness
You're wrong. I'm just busy
I have things to do
A career to achieve
A marriage to maintain
A family to support
I have no time for foolishness

Me looked sad but smiled
You try too hard
Relax. You'll have everything you need
Patience and love will get you there
Laugh along the way
I began to cry
I can't
I don't know how
Me wrapped her arms around I
Yes, you do.
Look inside you
The answers are there. Let them come.
I sobbed
But you're out there
You've deserted I.
Me looked I in the eyes
Hugging tighter
I never left you
Only stepped out to release you
And me
To let our happiness be free
We embraced again
When I opened my eyes
I laughed same as me.

Happiness

(also appeared in Standing: Poetry by Idaho Women and A New Beginning)

Happiness sneaked up
Wrapped her arms around me
Surprised me with her power
Snuggled me in her warmth
Enlightened me
Brought me out of the darkness
Allowed me to shine
I wasn't looking for her
Never expected her
Didn't recognize her
Wondered what the catch was
Questioned her
Pushed her away
Feared her
Accepting her meant letting go of the anger
Could I do that?
Happiness persisted through it all
Held me
Waited for me
Comforted me
And promised to stay
Even to grow
As long as I would let her
I smiled
Embraced happiness
And let her live around me
Inside my heart and mind
Let her build a barrier to protect me

Hiding

(also appeared on Associated Content)

The wall
It can't fall
Needing protection
Hiding from affection
Love is not accepted
Always rejected
Unable to give
Unwilling to receive
Hiding from all
Behind this wall
Created by pain
Allowing no gain
There's no trust
Only distrust
Making the wall strong
Seeing all that's wrong
Being alone
Allowing entrance to none
Unwilling to try
Refusing to cry
The wall grows
No one knows
Hiding behind this wall
What if it falls??

Tortured Mind

Trying to stay awake
Thinking of all I can't say
Trying to be there
Feeling apart from all
Now what do I do
Success used to come easy
Now I can't seem to find it at all
I do well at what I do, I think
But why don't I seem to make it
Why am I always fighting to do things right
I can't get it right
I struggle, I try, I put out the effort
But everything I do seems so wrong
Why when I'm happy are those with me miserable
Am I that different
I don't know where to turn
I don't know what to do
I don't know what is expected
I don't know what I want
I don't know what you want
I am so tired of trying
I am so tired of being
I am so lost
My thoughts collide as I ponder
What I am
Who I am
How I am
Who we are
What we are
What life means for me
What life means for us

What life means for anyone
I try and I try
No one I know is happy
Everyone seems to want something else from me
Everyone seems to want something they can't have
We struggle to achieve success, money, power
Thinking it all brings happiness
Yet it never does
Happiness is inside
We, no, I just seem to have misplaced it
Maybe we all have
Were our ancestors happy
Will our future generations find happiness
Or
Will they struggle to find it like we have for so long
My body needs to rest
My mind needs to free itself
My soul needs to relax
My heart needs to be safe
My personality needs to exist freely and openly
My life needs to be more than it is
What about you
Am I alone in needing peace, love, security, and happiness
Tell me am I alone
Are we really living or just existing
Think about it
Do you enjoy your life, really
There's work, family, stress, and responsibility
Do we take pleasure in any of it
Or

Do we just look for the money, the power, the recognition
Only to find the happiness doesn't follow
Will it ever be there

Or
Will we as a society keep making it
More and more impossible to find
Who knows
But promising
The future of our society, of our earth does not look
Think about it
Take a minute
Reflect
What is your greatest desire in life?
Where do you want to   be?
What do you want to do? Do you strive for these things?
Do you spend your life thinking
Tomorrow I will find happiness
Do you look inside and find what you have
To feel happy about
Do you want the same for those you love
It seems true happiness,
Lifelong happiness is the one thing
We can never seem to grasp
Keep striving and perhaps you will make it, perhaps I will
Perhaps we won't
But at least we can say we went for the real thing
The thing that really matters
Success, money, power, family, prestige, and recognition
What do they mean without happiness, I mean, really
Anything, nothing, who knows

Waiting

A life spent waiting

Waiting
To grow up
To feel respected
To achieve success
To be accepted

Waiting
For the right man
For the perfect relationship
For happiness
For life to feel fulfilling

Waiting
For the right time to speak
For the best words to say
For the appropriate way to express yourself
For your words to be accepted

Waiting
To feel good about yourself
To feel happy with yourself
To accept yourself
To love yourself

Waiting
For something
For everything
For anything
For nothing

Waiting
To share your happiness
To unload your burdens
To feel supported
To share your life

Waiting
For things to get better
For the hungry to be fed
For the world to find peace
For equality in the world

Waiting
To do the right thing
To find your path
To give of yourself
To reach new heights

Waiting
To be a better person
To find your place in the world
To change what you can
To create a life worth living

Waiting
To see you
To touch you
To hear you
To love you

Waiting
For the big things
For the little things

For what matters
For what means nothing

Waiting
What is a life spent waiting?

Success

Moving toward me
Feeling the excitement
Knowing change is near
Opening my heart
Clearing my mind
Accepting the success
My heart pounds
I won't turn away
I won't let fear stop me
I won't fail
I will smile
I will recognize the good
I will embrace change
Letting success dwell
In my heart
In my soul
In my life

Heels

Three inch shiny stilettos
Two and a half inch patent leather pointy toe pumps
Two inch floral linen peep toes
One and a half inch beaded sandals
One inch suede kitten heels
On the slide in
Foot tilts down
Ankle flexes
Calf muscle contracts
The thigh lengthens
Standing straighter
The legs look longer, leaner, stronger
Strength exudes from posture
Confidence settles into the soul
Coyness plays on the smile
Hope permeates the heart
Power emboldens thoughts
Determination resounds from each step
Feet follow the rhythm of movement
Bounce and flow combine
A strut tickles the toes
A little dance step taps from the ball of the foot
A pivot teases passers by
A lift and twist of the ankle demonstrates the weapon
A tiny kick into the air reveals the potential of threat
Red, brown, black, blue, green, yellow, white, pink
A color for every outfit
A heel from every mood
A heel for every event
A heel to add class to the simple
A heel to go from casual to professional

A heel to go from professional to evening out
A heel to add a touch of sexy
Put my foot in a heel
I'll show you just how staid – or sassy – I can be

Red

Red
Three inch patent leather stilettos scream power
Polished fingernails command attention
Matching toenails hint at playfulness
Lipstick invites your lips to touch mine
A splash of spice in the serious

Red
The dress that turned your head
                    And his before
                              And his before
The suit that exuded confidence when mine faltered
The tie between my breasts accentuating my femininity
The tie between your lapels proclaiming your masculinity
A splash of power in the professional

Red
The rose that survives the loss
The paper heart of young love with a tear in the cleavage
The silky lingerie long forgotten in the back of a drawer
The heart shaped balloon that slowly deflates as love ends
A splash of romance in the mundane

Red
Spicy
Strong
Romantic
Sexy
The color of power

Task List

I looked at my task list
Items populated it
To keep my day filled
To keep my mind occupied
To keep my body strong
To remind me what's important
To keep me focused
To list expectations
I read and reread that list
Something was missing
I felt it
I knew it
The incomplete items glared at me
The completed items were sparse
The unstarted items taunted
Still something was missing
My instincts knew it
My heart felt it
I stared and stared
Trying to locate the missing item
The words blurred
My heart skipped a beat
Suddenly I knew what was missing
My heart ached as I realized it
A tear slipped down my cheek
How could I have forgotten something so important
How could I have missed something so unforgettable
How could I have omitted something so wonderful
Suddenly I smiled
I laughed out loud at myself
Some things don't belong on a task list

Some things are too important for a task list
Some things are too unforgettable for a task list
Some things are too wonderful for a task list
Some things must just be a way of living
My forgotten item was one of those things
Love isn't a task to be checked off a list

Life

Moving through life
Feeling nothing
Feeling everything
Reality
Fiction
Perception
Fact
Thoughts moving through
Not stopping long enough to catch
Tempting
Stirring
Provoking
Fleeing
Words popping in
Not settling down
Stimulating
Disturbing
Escaping

Numbness

Numbness
Dominates my being
Invades my life
Conquers my mind
Freezes me
Stops my heart
Blocks my thoughts
Slowly kills me

Sleep

Night falls
Sleep envelops me
My eyes closed against the world
Darkness envelops my very being
I feel but can't see your arms around me
Snuggling down in the covers
My head resting on the pillow
Praying morning will never come
I pull my naked knees to my chest
Curled up in a fetal position
I feel safe and comfortable
If my eyes could just stay closed
If my body could just remain so relaxed
A ragged brown teddy bear clutched to my chest
My love curled up next to my back
Tracing an outline, making the two one
Warmth, love, and security surround me
I smile just before unawareness arrives
My eyes closed against all problems, against reality
My eyes closed against the world
Morning sneaks up on me
My eyes fight opening
I cuddle down in the covers feeling you behind me
Finally, I can fight it no longer
My eyes open to a bright new day
I see my teddy bear has found his way to the floor
I feel your back against mine
I know you've turned away without looking
I see the covers now askew around us
My pillow has pushed away from my head

I moan, half turning to see your peaceful, sleeping face
You turn and pull me to close to your warm body
Somehow you sense my need to shut out the world
I snuggle closer to you
I close my eyes willing night to last just a little longer
The peace, the serenity, the renewal
Sleep

Finding Truth

My body struggles
To hold onto health
To expel pain
To live each day
To find its truth

My mind struggles
To focus its purpose
To hold its thoughts
To reason its meandering
To find its truth

My heart struggles
To hold on to love
To contain its emotions
To understand its needs
To find its truth

My spirit struggles
To find meaning
To connect to mankind
To survive change
To find its truth

My being struggles
To live
To grow
To excel
To find truth

When I Feel

When I don't feel like myself
You remind me
Of not only who I am
But who I want to be

When I feel low
You hold me up
And push me higher

When I feel unsure
You show me not the answer
But challenge me to find it

When I feel lost
You show me not only where I am
But where I can go

When I feel unlovable
You not only love me
But force me to love myself

When I feel sad
You not only find my smile
But help me see true happiness

When I feel...
You're always there

Without You

Without you in my life...
I've lost
Without you to share my strife...
I've lost

Without you to care...
I've lost
Without you to share...
I've lost

Without you to understand...
I've lost
Without you to hold my hand...
I've lost

Without you to share my heart...
I've lost
Without you to share your heart...
I've lost

Without you to hold...
I've lost
Without you to grow old...
I've lost

Without you to ease my fear...
I've lost
Without you to be near...
I've lost

Without you to hug...

I've lost
Without you to return my hug…
I've lost

Without you to love…
I've lost
Without you to return my love…
I've lost

Without you to be my friend…
I've lost
Without you to stop our end…
I've lost

Without you…
I've lost

Have I lost, my friend?

Trust

Given
Taken
Nurtured
Cultured
Damaged
Repaired
Abused
Destroyed
-Trust-

Suffocating

Pressing down
Unable to breath
Gasping for air
Pain sets in

You walk away
My heart stops
My eyes fill with tears
Pain sets in

I know you're there
I'm scared
I need to let go
Pain sets in

Darkness surrounds me
Breathing stops
My heart stops
The pain ends

My eyes are open
They're staring without seeing
I'm cold but can't feel it
The pain is gone

Before... Now

Before
She couldn't let go
Now
There is no foe

Before
She only felt sad
Now
She can feel glad

Before
She always put herself last
Now
She can let go of the past

Before
Her life was unreal
Now
She can let herself feel

Before
She was trapped
Now
She feels her freedom is gift-wrapped

Before
The pain wouldn't go away
Now
Nothing can make her stay

Before

She had nothing to gain
Now
Never again

Before…
But not now

Freedom

Freedom from you
Sounded so sweet
Now I wish for a clue
How to feel complete

Freedom to be me
Was what I wanted
I don't feel free
Because I don't feel wanted

Freedom from your love
Felt so right
Now I look to the stars above
To get me through the night

Freedom is trapping me
By stopping my emotions
I'm not free
To feel affection

Give me back the freedom
To care....

Control Me

Silence me
With your sweet, urgent kiss
Hold me down
With your gentle, demanding caress
Tie me up
With your passionate, intoxicating embrace
Make me beg for more
With your charming, seductive words
Keep me on edge
With your teasing tongue
Demand obedience from my body
With your promise of addictive pleasure
Leave me longing
For more of your thrilling touch
Force me to the edge of ecstasy
With your undeniable talent
Make me want you more
With your denial of release
Give me the right reason
To relinquish my
Control

Control

I relinquish
Control
Or so you think
I give in
Hoping you'll believe you have
Control
It's always just enough
To keep you happy
Never enough for me
To feel controlled
Sometimes I wonder
What if I really gave you
Control
My heart races at the idea
I flirt with the concept
Even think it might provide relief
From this neverending need I feel
To control my every reaction
To control my every emotion
To control my every word
To control what everyone sees
To control every stray thought
To always be in complete
Control
I toy with relinquishing
Control
I give you a little more each day
Then jerk it back
Because I need
Control
More than you know

You never asked me for
Control
Not overtly anyway
Only by implication
Only by your reaction
To every time I take
Control
It's a struggle
That will never end
For ultimate
Control

Control Reclaimed

Enough
I take
Control
It's my life
I'll live it
If I make a mistake
I'll own it
If I succeed
I'll own it
You told me
How you wanted
Me to be
You showed me
What you considered appropriate
I listened
I paid attention
I tried to live
By your rules
I tried to adopt
Your rules as my own
I tried to believe
Your rules were better than mine
They stifled me
Left me gasping for air
Stopped my heart from beating
Bound my body with tension
Stomped my creativity into the ground
Ground my soul to dust
Melted my spirit
Left me for dead
Finally I screamed

Enough
Live by your rules
I'll live by mine
I take
Control

Sweet Seductive Strings

You whisper sweet, seductive words
Pulling the strings you attached long ago
Memories of your embrace stretch those strings
The distance between us matters not
As you pull first one string and then the next
Making my body, my heart, my mind dance to the rhythm
Of our sweet, seductive whisper
I pull against those strings
Fighting to stand on my own
Longing to free myself from the memory
Struggling to break those strings
The strings bounce back, strong, taut, ever resilient
I feel your gentle manipulation of those strings
I relax into your control
Feel you pull the strings this way and that
As you loosen your hold
I could run
Yet your hold on me is so strong
I barely notice the temporary release
Before you reassert your control
With a pull on those strings
As I greedily engorge on
As I readily surrender to
Your whisper of sweet, seductive words
Pulling on those strings you attached long ago

Or Don't

Touch me
>Or don't

Love me
>Or don't

Need me
>Or don't

Want me
>Or don't

Come to me
>Or don't

Stay away
>Or don't

Keep me company
>Or don't

Be my friend
>Or don't

Be my lover
>Or don't

Desire my presence
>Or don't

Welcome me
>Or don't

Shut me out
>Or don't

Splinter my heart
>Or don't

Say goodbye
>Or don't

Leave me
>Or don't

Stay with me

Or don't

Embrace me

Or don't

Kiss me

Or don't

Make love to me

Or don't

Build a future with me

Or don't

Create a past with me we'll leave behind

Or don't

Live in the present with me

Or don't

Run away

Or don't

Appreciate me

Or don't

Cherish me

Or don't

Make me your queen

Or don't

Treat me like a princess

Or don't

Call me a bitch

Or don't

Treat me like your whore

Or don't

Remember me

Or don't

Forget me

Or don't

Forgive me

Or don't

See me for who I am

Or don't
See only the image you've created of me
                                    Or don't
Blind yourself to my faults
                        Or don't
See only my faults glaring
                        Or don't
Grasp on to my good qualities
                        Or don't
Latch on to my bad qualities
                        Or don't
Give me everything I want
                        Or don't
Give me nothing I desire
                        Or don't
Hate me
        Or don't
Make your choice about me
                        Or don't

Naughty Teases Nice

My naughty teases my nice
Tickling her with ideas
Distracting her with fantasy
They play back and forth
Staid and sassy
Responsibility and desire
Expectations and pleasure
Pushing for more
Holding back
My naughty teases my nice
Bringing you near
Pushing you away
Whispering sweet sassiness in your ear
Leaving you wanting
Delivering cutting words with a smile
Leaving you wondering
Making promises of delight with sultry eyes
Refusing you my attention
Flashing you a mischievous half grin
Sashaying away
Showing you a glimpse of possibility
Keeping my distance
My naughty teases my nice
Reminding me that
Always, always, always
Naughty or nice
The choice is mine
But still
Always, always, always
My naughty teases my nice

You Believed

I smiled
You believed all was well
I laughed
You believed I had no sense of humor
I cried
You believed I was weak
I stood straight and tall
You believed I was strong
I told the truth
You believed I lied
I revealed my deepest feelings
You believed I was vulnerable
I gave you everything
You believed I was nothing
I opened my heart to you
You believed me broken
I screamed
You believed I had no voice
I went silent
You believed I told you all my secrets
I offered you paradise
You believed I delivered hell
I hid my truth from you
You believed you knew my very soul
I ran from you
You believed you owned me
I took back control of my life
You believed I couldn't survive without you
I acted...
You believed...
Sadly

We never inhabited the same truth at the same time

The End

(also appeared on Associated Content)

She sits staring
Seeing nothing
Feeling cold
Knowing she's old
A life of pain
So little to gain
She thinks of her life
She remembers her strife
Her children are grown
With lives of their own
They know nothing of her needs
As they move at their own speeds
She's all alone
Sad to the bone
Unable to care
Not caring to share
She knows she's dying
No way to change the lying
As they were her only happiness
She wants to end their sadness
She closes her eyes
As she cries
Shame for all her lies
Sadness for breaking all ties
Wishing she had never caused the pain
For her own selfish gain
Wanting better for her children
Until the very end
She feels so down
That she couldn't be around
She wants them to understand
Why she always had so much to demand
She opens her eyes

As she remembers all the lies
Her tears fall
As she remembers how she hurt them all
She stares into space
Not wanting to face
All she can't undo
All she can't make true
Time flies....
She dies....

Truly Alone

I am alone
My worst fear
My greatest desire
Encapsulated by family
Surrounded by friends
Embraced by others
And yet
I am alone
I am more alone
Than I've ever been
Though I'm rarely truly by myself
Though I'm in contact with the world constantly
Though friends and I interact daily
I am still alone
The disconnection inside
Pushes me to extremes
To feel connected
To feel part of those I love
To feel part of the world
To feel what I once felt
To reconnect with love
To reconnect with true companionship
To feel the intimacy of relationships
To recognize myself
And yet
When I'm honest
I am truly alone

Goodbye

Remembering unsaid goodbyes
And those spoken aloud
The most difficult word to utter
We stumble saying it
When it matters
And yet commonly we say it casually
Or do we?
We say
See you later
Talk to you soon
Call me
Peace
I'll call you
I love you
And any number of other words
To avoid actually saying
Goodbye
Goodbye represents endings
A sense of finality
No one wants to feel
Goodbyes are sometimes drawn out
With screened phone calls
Unreturned messages
Emails that linger unanswered in the inbox
Letters that dwindle to annual holiday cards
Avoiding places the person frequents
Holding on to tiny threads of possibility
For the relationship to somehow mend
Without the goodbye
Without the pain in knowing it's really over
And even without the goodbye

The relationship morphs
Never to be the same
Or it dissolves
Change is inevitable
But goodbyes don't have to come
Or do they?
Who ever wants to say
Goodbye
Who ever wants to hear
Goodbye
So we go about our days
Hoping a necessary goodbye
Will somehow turn into
Forgiveness
A brand new hello
And wondering
Will that
Fresh and exciting hello
Also end in
A spoken or silent
Goodbye

My Heart Broke Open

One day
My heart broke open
Pain poured out
Healing flooded in
Hatred evaporated
Acceptance rained in
Indifference disappeared
Passion appeared
Betrayal escaped
Trust squeezed in
Anger dissipated
Peace grabbed on
One day
My heart broke open
Love took up residence

Destiny Be Damned

Destiny showed up on my doorstep
Unannounced
Uninvited
Unwelcome
When I tried to shut her out
She put a foot in the door
When I tried to lock her out
She grabbed the knob and forced her way in
When she told me the truth I didn't want to hear
I spat in her face
When she showed me my path in life
I planted my feet and refused to move
When she shined light on the trail
I stomped my feet and pouted
Life would be what I wanted
I was in control
Destiny be damned

Destiny rapped on my window
I closed the curtain
Ignored her pleadings
To allow happiness in my heart
Shut out her efforts
To show me true love
When she pushed me to accept her way
I stuck out my tongue like a two year old
Why should I listen
I knew better
What my life should be
I was in control
Destiny be damned

When destiny whispered
That my life could be better
If I'd only accept her teachings
If I'd only let her lead me
If I'd only relinquish my viselike grip
I shut my heart
I closed my mind
I said
I trusted you once
Never again
The results pierced my heart with painful shards
I demand control
Destiny be damned

When destiny screamed
That I was lying to myself
That I was hiding from reality
That I was not really in control
I shook my head
I argued
I whined
You always get your way
After all
You're destiny
What chance do I have
What choice do I have
I take control
Destiny be damned

When destiny cried
In the face of my stubbornness
In the quake of my anger
In the quicksand of the life I created

I said
See I was right
You are weak
I'm stronger than you
I make better decisions
I am in control
Destiny be damned

The density has changed
So destiny says
What does that mean
I ask her quietly
Begging her to be kind to me
Begging her to embrace the best of me
Begging her to let me keep what's mine
Begging her to show me the path
Begging her to guide me to love
Begging her to do what I want
She shakes her head
She refuses to answer
She says I've treated her without respect
Now I'll have to wait
My mind reels with possibilities
I keep to myself
I fear sharing
I don't want to appear needy
I don't want to be thought weak
I don't want to be melodramatic
I don't want to face it all alone
I don't want anyone's help
When the possibilities invade my thoughts
She says
Any of the above may happen
Prepare yourself

Fight me now
If you can
Haven't you learned
I always win
So much for your control
So much for your demands
So much for every time you said
Destiny be damned

Friends, Enemies, Breasts

As a young girl
I eagerly anticipated your arrival
I watched for you daily
You would show the world my maturity
You took your time arriving
I exercised to encourage you
I flexed to make you noticeable
I wore a training bra on my flat chest to coach your growth
I imagined how you'd look

As a teenager
You embarrassed me
You just wouldn't stick out enough
You refused to enlarge
You brought on teasing nicknames
"Baby Boobs"
And I hated you for it
I willed you to grow
I begged you to grow
You stubbornly refused
I found ways to disguise you
I wore shirts and sweaters a size too large
I wore short skirts to draw attention away from you
I wore my coat all day
Other days
I pretended you were just want I wanted
I rebelled outwardly against my feelings about you
I disguised my disappointment in you
Deep inside though I knew my bravado was a lie
I imagined you how I wanted you to be
Just like…

Well, hers and hers and hers and…
But you were mine
And you had a mind of your own

As a young woman
I looked at you in the mirror
Resigned myself to your smallness
I hated you for not looking like I'd envisioned – dreamed
I drew attention away from you
To my legs
Always got them looking at my legs
And maybe they wouldn't notice your lack of size
I cursed your smallness
I failed to appreciate your symmetry
I failed to celebrate your firmness
I failed to recognize your perkiness
I made fun of you before others could
Then one day
Someone special uncovered you
Shushed my jeers at you with a kiss
Embraced you
Gave you a new nickname which also made me cringe
"Ozzie and Harriett"
-          For reasons known only to him
He caressed you
He appreciated you
He showed me your good qualities
He slipped a piece of ice into his mouth
And kissed you
You responded with a thrill and exaggerated perkiness
That spread through my body
And suddenly your size didn't seem so important
I stood straighter

I let you be who you were
But, alas, the moment ended

Time passed
Every time I cursed you
I remembered that not everyone found your size lacking
I embraced you
Showed you more proudly
A new man appreciated you
In his own way – different but just as loving
He caressed you
He held you
He declared you "just right"
He captured you in his mouth with joy
You responded with glee
I didn't question his desire for you
I reveled in the pleasure you brought him
I welcomed his approval
I grew to love you
I accepted your special attributes
I felt the pleasure of you

Suddenly
Without warning
You grew
You became womanly
At first I didn't believe
I waited for you to shrink
You created the curves
I always imagined
You stayed
But
Along with the size increase
Came days of soreness, of tenderness

Those days I cursed you again
The slightest touch felt like torture
Even clothing irritated you
But when I looked in the mirror
The new curves made me smile
And the pleasure you brought outweighed the pain

The doctor examined you
I'd yet to do so
Hadn't bothered to learn how
I was young
My only worries about you
Were your size and your potential for pleasure
The doctor declared you "perfect"
I liked the description
Even though it referred to you medically not aesthetically

Then one day
A hard spot appeared
It felt odd
It grew a bit uncomfortable
It didn't go away
The doctor grew concerned
I was only thirty-one
Too young for you to be sick
They placed you in a vise
Squeezed you
Told me to hold my breath
Unnecessary
I couldn't breathe anyway
What if...
I couldn't finish the thought
They took pictures of your tissue
Your density required a different type of picture

At long last
They declared you healthy
I finally let out my breath

I appreciated you
I loved you
I read how to take care of you
I changed my diet to keep you healthy
I examined you on a regular basis
Looked for changes
I grew to know you intimately
I looked at you in the mirror
But this time I didn't wish you larger
I only wished you healthy
I only wished you to remain "perfect"
I finally appreciated the beauty you possessed
I finally reveled in your firmness
I finally celebrated your perkiness
I finally realized you were never the problem
I enjoyed how you filled out my clothes
Was surprised when your size increased again
I took pleasure when you were
Caressed, touched, kissed, loved

You turned forty
Along with me
Time to get your picture taken again
Routine this time
No big deal
Joked with the technician
About the vise, the squeezing, the process
Laughed about the numbers on the machine's plate
Learned more about the process and the reading technique
Laughed about how each woman's experience is so different

Even joked about the fear a callback for a repeat test causes
Left in high spirits sure you were "perfect"
Two weeks later the phone rang
The words I remember
Density, left breast, changed, diagnostic
I know they were in a sentence, possibly two
Instinctively I touched you, searching
Instinctively I touch you now, searching
For a change I know I won't - can't - feel
It wasn't detectable in my last professional exam
It wasn't detectable in my last personal exam
I stand in front of the mirror
Staring at you
Willing you to be healthy
Loving you for all you bring me
Scared you'll betray me
Terrified you'll seek vengeance
For all those times
I didn't appreciate you
For all those times
 I actually hated you
For all those times
I willed you to be something you weren't
I cup my hand under you
I lift you to your former perky position
I don't mind that you're less perky
I love your size
I even love that slight sag you've developed
I love that you're real
I love that I've never falsified you
I love that you're unique
I love that you're all me
I love that you've been there without fail
No matter how I've treated you

I want you stay
I will protect you
I will love you
I will cherish you
I will appreciate you
Today, tomorrow, always
Please just don't betray me
Please just don't abandon me
Please just be healthy
Please just remain "perfect" in your imperfection

Known and Unknown

Thoughts never stop
Fears never wane
Dreams never leave
Feelings never pause
Collisions of past and present
Explode in possibilities
While the known dissolves
In to the unknown
And the unknown
Is swallowed by the known
Weakening the foundation
Giving way to the future
One way or another
The known and the unknown
Meld together without our permission
Creating a new known and unknown
Forcing us to move forward
Regardless of the past collision's warning
Of future collisions of past and present
The known colliding with the unknown
Has no choice but to happen
Again and again and again
As we grasp the future we desire
Or even the one we fear
So we close our eyes
Trying to pretend we don't need
The known and the unknown

Then Again

I want to say the words to you
I want to show you
I want to share with you
I want you to ask me
I want you to know
But then again I don't

I fear your response
I fear what it'll mean
I fear it's all a mistake
I fear if you know you'll hate me
I fear if you know you'll love me
But then again I don't

I need to take the risk
I need to know the answer
I need to know if there's a chance
I need to know if you even care
I need to know if it would change anything
But then again I don't

If you knew
What would you do
If I knew the outcome of you knowing
Would I have the courage to act
Would it change anything
I want to know
But then again I don't

Collision

The wall approaches at rapid speed
You don't slow down, you don't flinch
I watch from a distance
Dying to save you from yourself
Screaming unheard warnings
Waving unseen arms
You rush forward
Like you're blind to the wall's existence
I watch from a distance
Dying to save you from yourself
I beg and plead
I cry wasted tears
I jump up and down
You ignore all the warnings
Rushing toward a collision
I see so clearly approaching
I watch from a distance
Dying to save you from yourself
Just as once upon a time
I sped toward a flaming wall
Without slowing, without flinching
As you watched from a distance
Dying to save me from myself
Screaming unheard warnings
Waving unseen arms
I rushed forward
As if blinded to the wall's existence
As you watched from a distance
Dying to save me from myself
Begging and pleading
Crying

Jumping up and down
I ignored all the warnings
Rushed toward a collision
You saw so clearly approaching
You reached out
A gentle but strong set of arms to catch me
A grip as tender as a stalk of baby asparagus
I broke free
You couldn't save me from myself
That was my responsibility
I knew that then
Just as I know now
Saving you
Is your responsibility
Still I would
Save you from yourself
If only my warnings
Could stop your
Collision

Distract Me

I don't want to think
I don't want the truth
I don't want to know
I don't want an explanation
I don't want platitudes
Distract me
Keep my mind on the trivial
Give me a meaningless focused task
Tell me about the weather
Give me the details of the ball game
Tell me all the little nothings
Distract me
Don't leave me alone
Don't remind me of what I want to forget
Don't try to help me understand
Don't try to give me hope
Don't show me reality
For a little while
Distract me
Let me melt into fantasy
Let me pretend it's not real
Let me forget I hurt
Let me hide from the truth
Distract me
Eventually, I'll be ready
To face it all
But for now
Please, I beg you
Distract me
Please just
Distract me

Willful Blindness

Willful blindness makes the day go a lot smoother
I sent those words to explain how…
I've lived for years
Ignoring the obvious
Pretending life was just what I wanted
Blinding myself to the division between us
Willing reality to be what I dreamed
Wishing we were the image we projected
Wanting the connection we never quite found
Dreaming of what might have been
Fighting the truth of our life together
Molding me into the image you seemed to desire
Painting you into the image I wanted to see
Concealing the disconnection
Filling myself with images of what I want
Running from anything that didn't fit
Then one day
Willful blindness no longer made the day smoother
Not seeing revealed itself as dishonesty
My eyes opened to reality
My ears heard the silence sitting between us
My skin felt the sting of the façade we built
My tongue fought the words my heart needed expressed
My nose smelled the pain of the rotting foundation of us
My heart ached with longing for a love that uplifted
The pain of seeing what
Willful blindness hid
Is harder to feel than expected
Makes me long to return to the days when
Willful blindness worked…
When willful blindness failed

The truth bled through
My heart lost its ability to beat
My brain lost its ability to reason
Without willful blindness
All I had left
Was the empty shell of the girl I'd once been
Inhabiting a woman terrified of her own strength
As I began to step back into my true self
I realized that I risked everything
Unless I embraced
Willful blindness again
I tried
I really tried
Blinding myself became more difficult
As I learned there were people who liked me as is
                                        always had
As people embraced the me I cherished long ago
Then as I stepped into my true self
I saw the you I loved so long ago
Had also changed
Had become a shell of the man you were
Had stopped being your true self
Had given up crucial parts of yourself
Willful blindness has become a way of life for us both
Then the words tumbled out
Heartache ensued as the truth revealed itself
At first it seemed honesty might pull us together
But how much sacrifice of self is too much
At what point does it become destructive
At what point does it become unfixable
These questions float through my mind
As we flirt with fixing us
Isn't that what lead us here to begin with?
As we discuss ending us

Isn't fear of that what lead us here to begin with?
As I cry over potential lost
And you lament lost years
We see the issues with a clarity unseen before
And realize time doesn't necessarily mean happiness
And we wonder
Where we will end up
And how far we can take this conversation
Before we reach an actual conclusion
Before we finally realize
What we should've known all along
Willful blindness makes the day go a lot smoother
Willful blindness masks the truth
Willful blindness steals true intimacy
Willful blindness belies happiness
Willful blindness doesn't build a strong foundation

The Door

I opened the door
Right or wrong
Good or bad
Happy or sad
Smart or stupid
No hesitant peek through a sliver of open space
I threw it wide open
Held my breath
And waited

Would it have been easier
If you slammed the door in my face
A resounding thud on
Our past, present, and future
Quicker but not easier
Expected but unwanted
Decisive but no less painful
Understandable but devastating
Wise but heartbreaking

We met on the door's threshold
Clutched the frame of past experience
Tottered with the next step
Will you walk through
Will I
Will we balance on this thin strip of transition
Wary and vacillating
Ready to run back to the familiar
At the slightest provocation

More likely we'll take tentative steps

On either side of the door
Weigh words spoken
Then retreat to the threshold's safety
Hint at possibilities
One hand on the door's knob
Flirt with knowing each other intimately
Always keeping one foot on the threshold
Waiting, watching, wondering

Should this door be open
Or closed
Until the day someone makes a move
Merges past with present to move toward future
Blows the door off its hinges
Never to be closed
Or
Bolts it with an impenetrable lock never to open again

I opened the door

Three Out of Three

Would you love me still
If you could hear my thoughts
When they're at their darkest
When they're at their meanest
When they can't find love anywhere
If you felt my inner conflict
My need to be strong and independent
My fear of being controlled
My desire to control

Would you want me still
If you knew all my desires
Even the risqué ones
Even the ones I don't admit to myself
Even the ones I only want to fantasize
If my every thought and desire was on display
I show you all of the me I understand
But sometimes a part of me appears that I don't recognize
Then I pull away

Would you need me still
If you knew the depths of my selfishness
Sometimes I care more about my happiness than anything
Sometimes I really do want life to revolve around me
Sometimes I long to strike out against anything that impedes me
If I told you about the unfamiliar bits of me that appear uninvited
Are they real?
Or just fleeting thoughts?
How much can you handle?

If you still

Need me
Want me
Love me
Knowing all you know of me
And knowing there's a part me of I keep hidden inside
I'll give you my heart, my body, and my soul
If you'll give me room to understand myself
Cause three out of three wins every time

You for You

I liked you for you
Simple words
Beautiful words
Perfect words
You spoke them
I wanted to believe
I wanted to argue
No one liked me for me
Only what they wanted me to be
Yet
I couldn't argue
I couldn't quite believe either
Tears filled my eyes
Those words touched
A dormant place in my heart
One I hadn't noticed had gone dormant
I'm not even sure
I liked me for me
At least not then
I liked what I thought I could become
But
You liked me for me
I never saw that
Couldn't see that
Couldn't comprehend that possibility
How could you like me for me
When I didn't even like me for me
Yet
I know you spoke the truth
When you said
Those most beautiful, most musical words

I liked you for you

My Dock

My dock
Hours spent
Sitting on you alone
Staring at
Trees, poles, clouds reflected in the water's surface
The nearby building's reflection undulating
A fish taking a bite out of the cloud's reflection
A duck swimming through the leaves' reflection
The effect otherworldly
Reality absorbed in the reflection
Imagination escaped into the realm of possibility

My dock
Hours spent
Sitting on you
Youth my friend
Perhaps yours as well
My future endless
Imagining you would always be there
A string of people in and out of my life
Sharing my joy of you with them
Thinking each might be a lifetime friend or lover
Sharing special moments easily replaced by the next

My dock
Hours spent
Sitting on you alone
Your perfection not quite
Splinters protruded but unseen
Boards rough but intact and strong
A towel protected my bare legs, bare back, bare stomach

Your ruggedness, your roughness made me feel alive
No one understood the pleasure you brought me

My dock
Hours spent
Sitting on you alone
Knees to chest
Arms wrapped around knees
Rocking back and forth
Shutting out a heartache
Rewriting a betrayal
Shedding tears
Each tear too small to even splash
Disappearing into the water beneath
Wishing those waters could absorb
My sorrows
My shame
My mistakes
My pain
So they would dissipate
So they would drown in the depths beneath you
Maybe they did
Perhaps my tears
Contributed to your demise

My dock
Hours spent
Sitting on you alone
The decisions I made
Sunning, studying, thinking, plotting, planning
Wanting to be different
Wanting the world
Wanting everything I thought would bring happiness
Wanting to feel whole again

Wishing I could undo my mistakes
Wishing I could forget
Wishing I was what *he* needed
Wishing I was someone *he* could love
                    Whoever *he* happened to be

My dock
Years later I returned
Excited to sit on you again
Appreciating this place
Where I'd found new life
Where I'd found my balance every time I lost it
Where I'd given my dreams free reign to explore
Where I'd always felt most like myself
Whoever that was in the moment

My dock
The dance we shared
Swaying against life's ups and downs
Your strong and rhythmically flexible structure
Never failed to embrace my mood
Never failed to hold the weight of my emotions
Never failed to rock away my unhappiness
Never failed to leave me with hope

My dock
I stood above you
Poised to climb down the metal ladder
Looking down
My heart broke
My voice froze
I stared
At rotted boards
Holes larger than my leg

Rusted bolts
Splinters sticking straight up
Splits in your demeanor

My dock
A barricade
Forbids access to you
I started to ignore it
I wanted to ignore it
But life's experience made me wary
I imagined
The slow destruction to your structure
Tears filled my eyes
Remembering times past
Realizing your holes
Mirror my heart
Your splinters
Mirror my soul
Your decay mirrors my being
Your demise
Mirrors the toll
Life has taken on the girl who loved you so much
Yet I want to sit on you
Take the risk
Regret still that I didn't
I would've way back when...
I wasn't scared then
My need for you too great
But I've changed
I've become
Respectable
Cautious
Scared
The very person

I swore I'd never be
You letting me down would be too much, too final
You not holding me would end the dream
You failing beneath me would be a reality too harsh to bear
Best to leave my memories of you untainted

My dock
A sign
Warns of the dangers
Of experiencing you
No sign
Warns those nearing me of the dangers
Of experiencing me
Of the holes
Of the weaknesses
Of the splinters
Of the rot
Visited upon my heart
Visited upon my soul
Visited upon my being
Visited upon the girl I was then

My dock and I
Aged the same
In disrepair
No longer recognizable as we knew one another
Time eroded
Our surface
Our strength to hold the weight of others' needs
Our flexibility to right ourselves after an injury
Our wholeness to tolerate the unfair abuses of outsiders
Our naiveté that we would always be kept unchanged,
whole
Perhaps who we were has become

Too much work
Unappreciated
Irrelevant
Lost to today and tomorrow
Only important to yesterday – to memories
A falling apart college campus dock that never let me down
Despite my imperfections
And the woman who loves you still
Imperfections and all
You were always and always will be
My dock

I Hate You:
A Love Poem

I hate you
For making me see
What I didn't want to acknowledge

I hate you
For pointing out
The reality of my life

I hate you
For opening wounds
I'd long considered healed

I hate you
For making me face
My responsibility in creating my circumstances

I hate you
For showing me
The changes I made to be loveable were unnecessary

I hate you
For making me realize
People who really love me prefer my true self

I hate you
For breaking the mask
I'd so carefully created and proudly worn

I hate you
For revealing

The longing in me to be my self

I hate you
For awakening
My hunger to be loved for myself

I hate you
For making me question
Everything I thought I knew, just everything

I hate you
For coercing me into
Believing in my independent nature again

I hate you
For making me recognize
That I'd forgotten my strength lies within

I hate you
For giving me a reason
To want something different in my life

I hate you
For uncovering
My long forgotten courage

I hate you
For showing me
Some people enjoy my sense of humor

I hate you
For making me crave
The joy of laughter

I hate you
For saying the words
That forced me to face the truth

I hate you
For insisting
I unhide what I'd hidden

I hate you
For destroying
My delusion of perfection

I hate you
For reminding me
Who I once was

I hate you
For not enlightening me sooner
That I was worthwhile

I hate you
For making me feel
Long denied emotions

I hate you
For going just far enough
To make me want more

I hate you
For reviving
Dormant fantasies

I hate you
For thawing

Long frozen passions

I hate you
For flaunting a life
That could never be mine

I hate you
For unearthing
Long buried pleasures

I hate you
For bringing
Happiness back into my life

I hate you
For loving me for me
When I didn't know how

I hate you
For making me
Love me for me

I hate you
For making me
Love you

Me

Who shall I be?
Only me
Changing as I learn

Learned

I have learned
When my heart speaks, to listen
When my soul doubts, to question
When my mind screams, to hesitate
When my body tingles, to answer
I have learned
No one can ask my questions
No one can answer my soul
No one can guide my heart
No one can offer me solace
No one can provide me life
No one can love me
Like I can
I have learned
That until I accept me
All of me, the naughty and the staid
I have nothing to offer
To the world
To anyone
To you
To me

Sound

I heard a sound
One I didn't quite believe came from me
It echoed
An assertive tone
A confident voice
A soothing inflection
Uninhibited laughter
Pleasure oozed between the syllables
Love sheltered the words
Boldness lingered between the sentences
Optimism melded the paragraphs
The sound projected with gentle forcefulness
Teasing
Flirting
Joking
Enticing
Inviting
All came from me
The sound exuded
Power
Strength
Acceptance
Happiness
Honesty
All expressed by me
The sound gave compassionate voice to
Sobs
Heartache
Betrayal
Loss
Grief

All genuinely released by me
The sound stepped into its place with pride
Growth
Beauty
Love
Esteem
Confidence
All glowed through the sounds I made
I heard a sound
One I didn't quite believe came from me
The sound of a woman who loves herself

Self Portrait in Words

Words paint me for you
A sketch of half-revelations in cryptic lines
Broad brush strokes of an acceptable image in lyrical verses
Sculpted sentences expose myriad aspects of me
A collage of images past and present meld into paragraphs
Folds in origami hint at the secrets hiding in my heart
Strokes of red denote the passion I feel
Fine lines of black conceal the darkness in my thoughts
A touch of brilliant yellow shines upon the happiness I fear
Dots of brown mar the sunshine with my sadness
Swirling blue intimates the depths of my true nature
A smattering of green symbolizes the growth of my soul
Shining white forces light on the innocence I once held
Pink hides in the shadows exposing my femininity
Purple peeks from the edges offering a glimpse of attitude
Gold crowns my need for the spotlight
Silver highlights my penchant for angelic expectations
A fine canvas both concealing and revealing
The truth of me bleeds through
Despite my best efforts to hide it
Each new word
Another outline sketched
Another brush stroke
Another sculpture
Another collage
Another origami
Toward my
Self portrait in words

Reflections in Silhouette

Reflections in silhouette
The girl I once was
Flattened by heartache
Darkened by betrayal
A dimension lost in the voids
Light reflects behind me
Highlighting the outline of
The woman I long to be
I look for a way to
Fill in the dimensions
Find the inner light
Allow my heart to love
Allow my soul to absorb
Allow my body to be complete
Looking out at what was
Searching for what is
Reaching for what could be
The girl in me breathes
Life into the woman I've become
Urging me to see
More in me than
Reflections in silhouette

ABOUT THE AUTHOR

T. L. Cooper grew up on a farm in Tollesboro, Kentucky. She earned her Bachelor of Science degree from Eastern Kentucky University in Richmond, Kentucky. Her poems, short stories, articles, and essays have appeared online, in books, and in magazines. Her books include a novel, *All She Ever Wanted*, and a book of poetry, *Love in Silhouette*. When not writing, she enjoys yoga, golf, and traveling. Currently, she lives in Albany, Oregon. To learn more, visit www.tlcooper.com.

www.ingramcontent.com/pod-product-compliance
Lightning Source LLC
Chambersburg PA
CBHW051833040426
42447CB00006B/502